A FOCUS ON...

DEATH

By
John Wood

©2018
Book Life
King's Lynn
Norfolk PE30 4LS

ISBN: 978-1-78637-215-4

Written by:
John Wood

Edited by:
Kirsty Holmes

Designed by:
Evie Wright

A catalogue record for this book
is available from the British Library

PHOTO CREDITS

**Abbreviations: l-left, r-right, b-bottom,
t-top, c-centre, m-middle.**

Front Cover – Olesia Bilkei. 2 – Serg64. 3 – toyotoyotoyo. 4l – Ints Vikmanis, 4m – nature photos, 4r – dezi. 5 – Reddogs. 6 – topnatthapon. 7 – Robert Hoetink. 8 – Alzbeta. 9 – Pozdeyev Vitaly. 10 – Halfpoint. 11 – Nailia Schwarz. 12 – Duplass. 13 – VTT Studio. 14 – Hannamariah. 15 – wattana. 16 – Monkey Business Images. 17 – Asier Romero. 18 – LilKar. 19 – Andrey_Popov. 20 – Joanna Dorota. 21 – altanaka. 22 – Marc Bruxelle. 23 – toyotoyotoyo.

Images are courtesy of Shutterstock.com.
With thanks to Getty Images, Thinkstock Photo and iStockphoto.

DEATH

Words that look like this can be found in the glossary on page 24.

What Is Death?

Every person, plant and animal is alive. But eventually, something happens to all living things. They will stop moving, breathing or eating. This is called 'death'.

Living Things

Most of the time people and animals die when they get old, after a long life. Sometimes they might have a bad **accident** or become very sick.

"Our dog was very old. One day I came home from school and Mum told me he had died. He died because he was so old."

Kurt – aged 7

What Happens When People Die?

Death isn't like sleeping, although it might look like it. People who are dead won't wake up again. They are not scared and they do not worry about anything.

Being dead isn't painful at all. When someone is dead, we often say they are 'at **peace**'.

Saying Goodbye

When people die, we say a special goodbye to them. Different people and **religions** have different ways of saying goodbye.

Christianity

Buddhism

Judaism

You might want to talk to your family about their **beliefs**. Ask them how they would say goodbye to a person who has died.

Talking about Your Feelings

After a loved one's death, we deal with lots of different feelings. This is called **grieving**.

"When my uncle died we looked at his photos. I felt sad and had to ask Mum lots of questions." Amena – aged 7

When a person dies, you might not know what to do, and that is OK. Just remember, it is important to talk about how you are feeling.

You Might Feel Sad

You may feel like you want to cry all the time, especially when you think about the person you love.

"I cry when we walk past my grandma's old house. Dad says it is OK to cry."

Marek – aged 7

It might help to draw a picture of your loved one, or to draw how you are feeling. You could also keep a diary.

Diaries and drawings are a good way to show how you feel.

You Might Feel Angry

You might feel angry or frustrated and this is fine. It is important not to shout at or hit other people, though.

"I get angry when I think about death. It's not fair.

I sit in the garden on my own until I feel better."

Chloe – aged 9

It might help to run around or kick a ball when you feel especially angry. You might want to talk to people, but it is OK. if you want to be left alone, too.

You Might Feel Lonely

You might miss your loved one and want to talk to them, even though they are not there.

"My grandad was very old. He gave me his medals from the war before he died." Jon – aged 8

It might help to write a letter to your loved one, and say all the things you want to say to them.

You Might Feel Scared

Maybe you feel scared or worried. It is important to share what you are worried about. You could talk to someone you trust about this. They will understand.

"Mum says I don't need to be scared when people die.

She says it's a normal part of life."

Farhana – aged 6

Sometimes it might help to speak to a **counsellor**. Counsellors are very good at helping you work out your feelings.

A Counsellor

Understanding Other People's Feelings

It is important to remember that other people grieve too.

"Dad cried a lot when Auntie died. I asked him if he was alright and he told me he needed time to cry because he was sad."

Charlotte – aged 7

We need to help each other when we grieve. We can cope with these new feelings by sharing them with loved ones.

Remembering Those We Love

We all have our own way of remembering those we love. Maybe you remember your loved one by drawing pictures of them, or writing stories about them.

Some people visit their loved one's grave.

GLOSSARY

accident   something bad that happens by chance

beliefs   something you think is true, even if you can't see, hear or touch it

counsellor   someone trained to help people with feelings and personal problems

grave   a place where someone's body is buried which often has a headstone with information about the person

grieving   coping with difficult feelings when someone you love has died

peace   without disturbance or suffering

religions   the belief in and worship of a god or gods

INDEX